The Christmas Hippo

Lisa E. Williams

WestBow Press books may be ordered through booksellers or by contacting:

WestBow Press
A Division of Thomas Nelson & Zondervan
1663 Liberty Drive
Bloomington, IN 47403
www.westbowpress.com
844-714-3454

Because of the dynamic nature of the Internet, any web addresses or links contained in this book may have changed since publication and may no longer be valid. The views expressed in this work are solely those of the author and do not necessarily reflect the views of the publisher, and the publisher hereby disclaims any responsibility for them.

Any people depicted in stock imagery provided by Getty Images are models, and such images are being used for illustrative purposes only.
Certain stock imagery © Getty Images.

ISBN: 978-1-4497-2474-0 (sc)
ISBN: 978-1-4497-8056-2 (e)

Library of Congress Control Number: 2012916951

Print information available on the last page.

WestBow Press rev. date: 03/04/2021

WESTBOW
PRESS®
A DIVISION OF THOMAS NELSON
& ZONDERVAN

To Ken, my page-turning partner in this book called, "Life"

Jeremiah 29:11

To Gabriela, Logan, and Brandon

Remember "Give all your worries and cares to God,
for He cares about you." 1 Peter 5:7 (NLT)

L.W.

To Terry, the Captain of my heart ~ I love sailing thru
life with you, Kristi my beautiful baby girl & Daisy my
precious dog ~ you are the loves of my life ~ S.B.D.

To God be the Glory

It was the much long awaited time of the school year.

The class Christmas party was finally here.

Through the cookies, the juice,
and the candy galore,

Only the angels could have known
what was really in store.

For 'twas at that party
that two girls asked, wide-eyed,

"Can Kay spend the night?"
"Sure, why not?" I replied.

See, Kay was soon
moving
to a town far away.

And, so plans were
made that
she'd come the
next day.

When I brought both girls home,
they squealed with delight

As I told them our plans to
go caroling that night.

Once we were home, the two girls laughed and played,

While I thumbed through songbooks and had copies made...

How could I have known
that just miles away

A kind hearted bus driver
was ending his day?

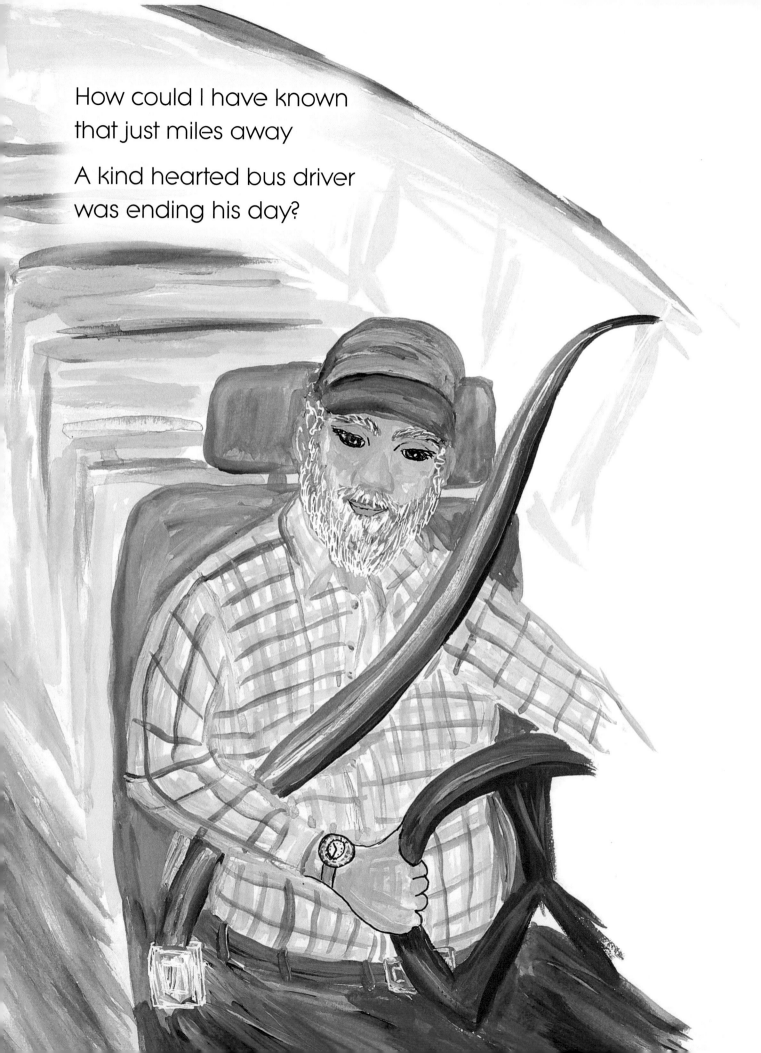

Picking up old gum wrappers,
going through every seat,

When he noticed a hippo
right there at his feet.

He picked up the hippo and
thought with dismay,

"This is Kay's little sister's, but
they're moving away."

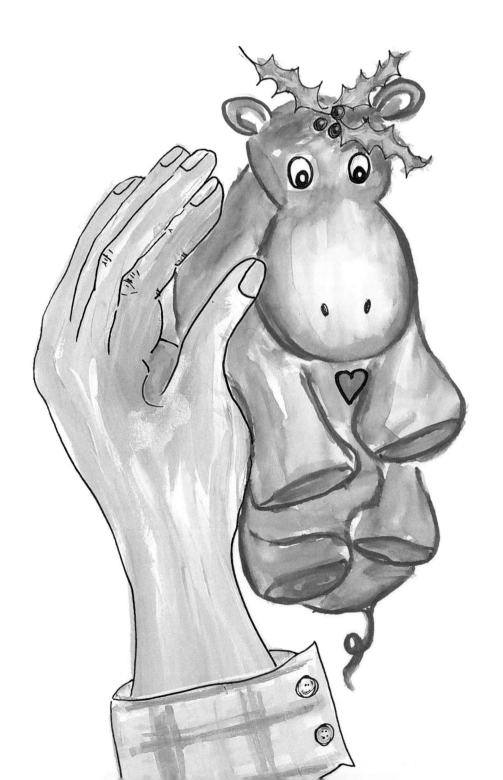

With hopes to return it,
he stopped by her home,

But found the house empty
and very alone.

He saw the word, "sold," where the sign said, "for sale"

Then he thought he could send it to her in the mail

He called up the school,
but Christmas break had begun.

The office was closed.
Nothing more could be done.

School Closed
Christmas Break
Classes Start Jan. 3

He arrived at his home
feeling just a bit down.

And told his wife all about
the small hippo he'd found.

He explained his desire
to return it to the child.

Then his wife took his hand,
and she said with a smile,

"Dear, why don't we pray?
God surely will know

How to reunite a girl
with her long lost hippo."

So, they both closed their eyes
and together, heads bowed,

Asked God to rejoin child
and hippo somehow.

Well, just hours after that on
that cold winter's night,

He opened the door
to a miraculous sight.

Carolers singing
of God's love and joy

Celebrating the birth
of His Sweet Little Boy!

And there on his stoop,
to his utter surprise,

Was Kay singing sweetly
right in front of his eyes!

He quick grabbed
the hippo,
embraced her
with love

Wished her a
blessed Christmas
and looked up
above.

"God you care 'bout our hippos.
My mind cannot conceive

How much more you'll provide
if we'd only believe."

"Thank you Lord Jesus for
answering my prayer.

Thank you for Christmas hippos
to remind us You care."

Lisa E. Williams has been married to her husband, Ken for 20 years. They often laugh at the antics of their three children as they build their life together in Delaware. In addition to being a wife and mother, Lisa is also a licensed clinical social worker who passionately enjoys serving her community. Lisa's ministries include singing on the praise team, community outreach development, and teaching Sunday School. As one who values the importance of children having a relationship with God, it is her hope that through The Christmas Hippo, young readers will begin to understand how much God loves and cares for them.

Stacie Desautels is the colorful, whimsical artist of Daisy DeZigns Art Studio in Salisbury, Maryland. Her style is fresh and full of swirling colors designed to delight the viewer. A two-time breast cancer survivor, Desautels has a true appreciation for the magical moments and miracles that occur everyday. Stacie recognizes her talent and passion for painting as a gift from God, the Master Artist, to be used to touch hearts, inspire changed lives and bring Glory to God. Desautels is known for her eccentric illustrations created for the Wicomico County Autumn Wine Festival each year, Blue Bear Finds a Rainbow picture book, numerous children's murals, and her *Mindful Moments* inspirational "Thought for the Day" cards. Visit Stacie at www.daisydezignsartstudio.com.

Printed in the United States
by Baker & Taylor Publisher Services